WHAT YOU NEED TO KNOW ABOUT
CANCER

BY CHRIS FOREST

CONSULTANT:
MARJORIE J. HOGAN, MD
UNIVERSITY OF MINNESOTA
AND HENNEPIN COUNTY MEDICAL CENTER
ASSOCIATE PROFESSOR OF PEDIATRICS
AND PEDIATRICIAN

CAPSTONE PRESS
a capstone imprint

Fact Finders Books are published by Capstone Press,
1710 Roe Crest Drive, North Mankato, Minnesota 56003
www.capstonepub.com

Library of Congress Cataloging-in-Publication Data
Cataloging-in-Publication data is on file with the Library of Congress.
ISBN 978-1-4914-4831-1 (library binding)
ISBN 978-1-4914-4899-1 (paperback)
ISBN 978-1-4914-4917-2 (eBook PDF)

Developed and Produced by Focus Strategic Communications, Inc.
    Adrianna Edwards: project manager
    Ron Edwards: editor
    Rob Scanlan: designer and compositor
    Mary Rose MacLachlan: media researcher
    Francine Geraci: copy editor and proofreader
    Wendy Scavuzzo: fact checker

Photo Credits
2014 The Skin Cancer Foundation, 19; Alamy: Keith Morris, 5; Alex's Lemonade Stand Foundation, 29 (middle); Glow Images: Corbis/Wolfgang Flamisch, 20; iStockphoto: MachineHeadz, 12 (bottom); Newscom: Blend Images/ERproductions Ltd, 12 (top), UPI/Bill Greenblatt, 28 (top); Science Source: 3D4Medical, 8, CAMR/A. Barry Dowsett, 6 (inset), David Scharf, 6 (back), Girand, 18, Larry Mulvehill, 11 (right), Steve Gschmeissner, 15, Sue Ford, 7, Zephyr, 16; Shutterstock: A and N Photography, 13, Alex Luengo, 17, Alexander Raths, 10, Andrey Starostin, 9 (bottom right), Binh Thanh Bui, 9 (bottom left), Bullstar, 4 (right), everything possible (background), back cover and throughout, frantab, 21, isak55, cover (top), 1 (top), 3 (back) and throughout, Jovan Mandic, 22, Jovan Vitanovski, cover (bottom), 1 (bottom), Kumpol Chuansakul, 11 (left), Monkey Business Images, 4 (left), Peter Zijlstra, 9 (top middle), PhotoSkech, 23, prudkov, 25, spafra, 9 (top right), Suslik1983, 9 (top left), Vectomart, 24, vetpathologist, 14, vinz89, 29 (top), wavebreakmedia, 27; SuperStock: Fancy Collection, 26

Printed in China
042015   008831LEOF15

TABLE OF CONTENTS

CHAPTER 1
WHAT IS CANCER?

A doctor in a hospital tests new medicines on patients. A researcher in a laboratory begins work on a new treatment. A group of people walk 26 miles (42 kilometers) together to help raise awareness. Three siblings open a lemonade stand to earn money for a cure.

▼ Doctors test new cancer medicines.

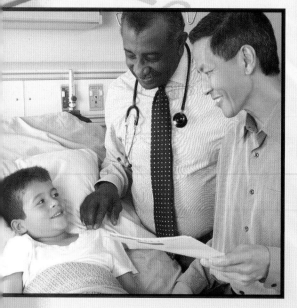

▲ A scientist searches for cancer treatments.

What do these people have in common? They are all working to find a way to cure cancer. Their efforts will help patients fight the disease. They will also help to find newer and better ways to put an end to cancer.

▲ People walk and run to raise money for cancer research.

DEFINING CANCER

Most people think of cancer as one disease. It is really a group of diseases that affects the **cells** of the body. Cells are the building blocks of every part of the body. Cells usually grow in the body and are replaced as they wear out.

A healthy body can start and stop cell growth. But sometimes, the body is unable to stop cell growth. This illness is called cancer. When a person has cancer, cells in a part of his or her body grow and divide much faster than usual.

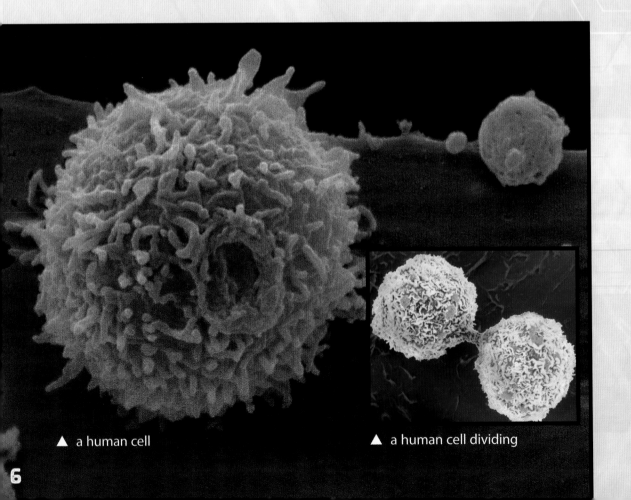

▲ a human cell

▲ a human cell dividing

At times these cells can grow into a mass of cells. This is sometimes called a **tumor**. This uncontrolled cell growth can cause damage to cells in **tissue** and destroy normal cells.

▼ damaged cells in tissue

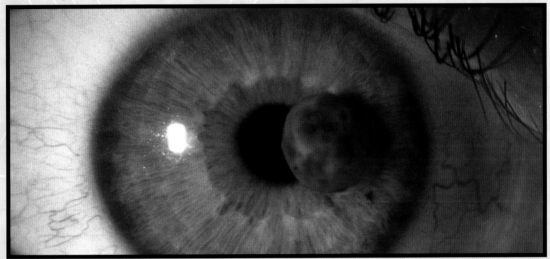

cell—the smallest unit of a living thing

tumor—an unhealthy mass of cells in the body

tissue—a mass of cells that form a certain part or organ of a person, animal, or plant

CAUSES OF CANCER

Cancer affects many people. In the United States, about one and a half million new cases are **diagnosed** each year. Nearly 16,000 of those cases are in children. Worldwide about 160,000 new cases of cancer are diagnosed in children under age 15 each year.

No one knows what causes this cell growth. But two facts are certain. First, cancer is not a germ that can be passed through the air. Second, no one can catch cancer from another person.

Scientists think that cancer can be caused by damage to a person's **DNA**.

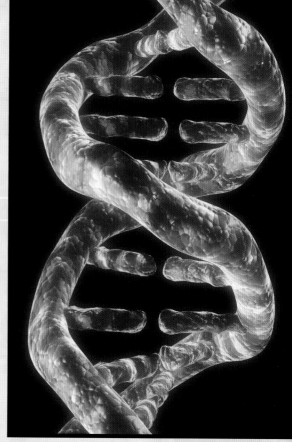

▲ human DNA

This is the material in a person's **genes** that makes each person one of a kind. Many things can cause this damage. Some causes might come from the environment. For example, chemicals in the ground, air, or water might cause cancer.

diagnose—to find the cause of a problem

DNA—material in cells that gives people their individual characteristics; DNA stands for deoxyribonucleic acid

gene—a tiny unit of a cell that determines the characteristics that a baby gets from his or her parents

Habits that people may have can also lead to cancer. These habits can include smoking, eating many unhealthy foods, drinking too much alcohol, and lack of exercise. Sometimes the genes a person gets from a parent can make him or her more likely to get a certain type of cancer. A person might get cancer later in life if the genes change or are damaged.

▲ blueberries

▲ spinach

▲ tomatoes

HEALTH FACT

Scientists think some foods help prevent cancer. These foods include apples, blueberries, cherries, cranberries, grapefruit, grapes, broccoli, dark leafy greens, squash, tomatoes, dry beans and legumes, flax seed, garlic, green tea, soy, walnuts, and whole grains.

▲ broccoli

▲ cherries

CHAPTER 2

DIAGNOSING CANCER

Doctors use tests to find out if a person has cancer.
Diagnosing cancer is the first step in treating it.

Special doctors focus on the treatment and care of cancer.
They can come up with a plan for dealing with cancer.

▲ A doctor discusses test results and a treatment plan for cancer with her patient.

Different tests can help diagnose cancer. A blood test can show if there are cancer cells in the blood.

Other times, doctors use X-rays to tell if a person has cancer. One X-ray machine is called a **CT/CAT scan**. The machine can take 3-D images of a person. This helps a doctor see tissues inside the body.

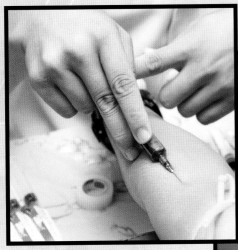

▲ A blood test can be used to diagnose cancer.

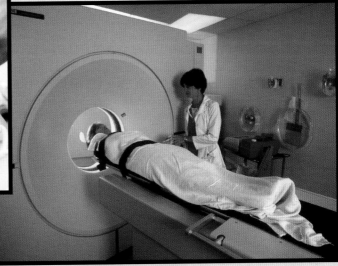

▲ Doctors also use CT scans to find out if a patient has cancer.

HEALTH FACT

In 1971 Godfrey Hounsfield developed the first CT scanner. He received the Nobel Prize in 1979 for developing the machine.

CT/CAT scan—an X-ray machine that takes pictures inside a person; CT stands for computed tomography

OTHER WAYS TO DIAGNOSE CANCER

Another way to tell if someone has cancer is by using an **MRI**. This machine can find cancer in tissues that other machines might miss.

HOW DOES AN MRI WORK?

An MRI machine looks like a long tube. Patients are injected with a dye. This dye helps organs show up better when the machine scans them. An MRI has a very large magnet. It weighs more than 1 ton (0.9 metric tons)! It uses the magnet to take pictures. The MRI shows amazing images of the inside of the body.

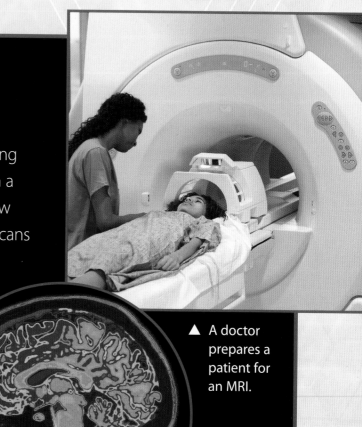

▲ A doctor prepares a patient for an MRI.

◀ an MRI scan showing the brain

When a doctor finds a tumor, he or she must determine if it is cancerous. To do this a doctor may take a sample of the cell tissue. This tissue is later studied, sometimes under a microscope. This process is called a **biopsy**.

▲ Doctors use microscopes to examine biopsies.

ZACH'S DIAGNOSIS

When Zach was 2 years old, his parents noticed he was not eating or sleeping well. His stomach stuck out more than normal. His parents took him to a doctor. Doctors ran tests to help find out what was wrong. The tests used X-rays and CT scans together. The doctors found a tumor, and a biopsy showed it was cancerous. Zach's doctors were able to use different treatments to shrink the tumor. Doctors often use several treatments in cancer care.

MRI—a machine that uses a magnet to help take a picture of the inside of a person; MRI stands for magnetic resonance imaging

biopsy—taking a sample of tissue to determine if it has a disease

TYPES OF CANCER

There are different types of cancers. Some cancers begin in **organs**, **glands**, and on the skin. Others form in tissues that join parts of the body, such as muscles, bones, or blood vessels. Some grow in the blood system.

Cancers that affect organs include lung cancer, skin cancer, colon cancer, and breast cancer. Different cancers affect organs in different ways. This means lung cancer acts differently than colon cancer.

Cancers that form in the blood and bones are called leukemia. People who have this disease have white blood cells that do not act properly. Normal white blood cells help fight illnesses. Leukemia causes the body to have too many white blood cells that do not work the way they should.

▼ Leukemia cells are shown in a blood sample. People who have leukemia cannot fight infections well.

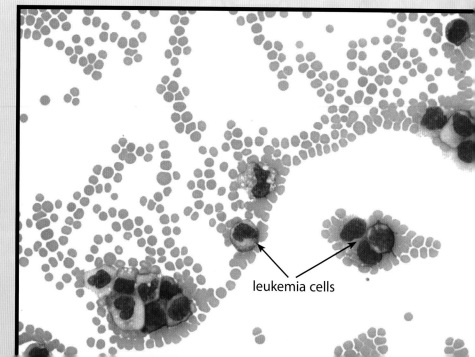

leukemia cells

ALIJAH'S FIGHT WITH LEUKEMIA

When Alijah was 2 years old, he suddenly stopped walking. Instead, he returned to crawling. After many tests, doctors were puzzled. Then they did a biopsy and found that Alijah had a type of leukemia. Alijah's leukemia could be treated with medicines. It had an 80 percent cure rate. The treatments took months, but they were successful. In time, Alijah learned how to walk again.

Lymphoma is a cancer that forms in the glands of the **lymph system**. It occurs when white blood cells multiply very quickly. These cells help the body fight infection. But too many of these cells can make you sick.

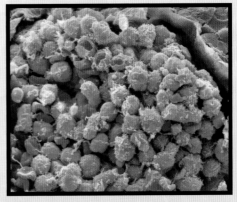

▲ lymphoma cancer cells

Parts of the Body Affected by the Lymph System			
tonsils	liver	lymph nodes	skin
heart	bone marrow	lungs	
spleen	intestines	thymus	

organ—a body part that does a certain job, such as the heart or lungs

gland—an organ that either produces chemicals or allows substances to leave the body

lymph system—a body system that helps keep body fluids balanced and fight infections

CHAPTER 3
TREATING CANCER

After a person is diagnosed with cancer, doctors must find a way to treat it. First they need to see where the cancer is. Doctors locate the cancer using different tools, such as MRI or CT scans.

▼ This MRI scan of the brain shows cancer cells.

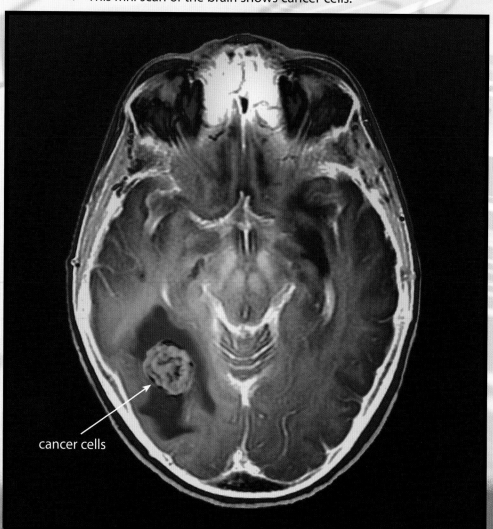

cancer cells

Next the doctors must figure out how far the cancer has spread. When they find out, they label it with a stage. Cancers run from Stage 1 to Stage 4. Stage 4 cancers have spread the most.

Once doctors know the cancer's type, location, and stage, they make a plan to treat it. They may use surgery, chemicals, or radiation. Often they use more than one kind of treatment.

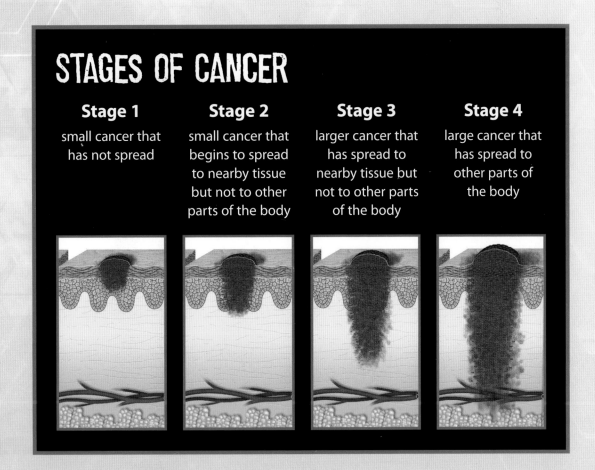

STAGES OF CANCER

Stage 1
small cancer that has not spread

Stage 2
small cancer that begins to spread to nearby tissue but not to other parts of the body

Stage 3
larger cancer that has spread to nearby tissue but not to other parts of the body

Stage 4
large cancer that has spread to other parts of the body

SURGERY

Surgery is the most common way to treat cancer. If the cancer has not spread, surgery is one of the best ways to remove it. Depending on the type of cancer surgery, doctors may give patients medicine to make them sleep during the operation.

Sometimes cancer is located on the skin. The doctor can give the person medicine to make that part of the skin numb. Then the cancer can be removed.

Doctors try to remove all cancer cells during the surgery. This can stop cancer from spreading. Sometimes doctors use surgery and other cancer-fighting methods.

▼ cancer on the ear

DIFFERENCES BETWEEN NONCANCEROUS AND CANCEROUS MOLES

Sometimes a doctor will remove growths that may not yet show signs of cancer. For example, if the doctor thinks a mole might turn into cancer, it may be removed.

Noncancerous Mole   **Cancerous Mole**

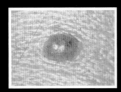 both halves are the same   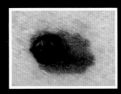 both halves are not the same

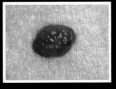 borders are even   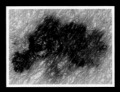 borders are uneven

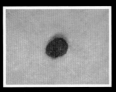 one shade of color   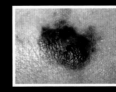 two or more shades of color

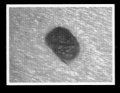 smaller than ¼ inch   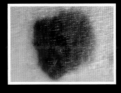 larger than ¼ inch

CHEMOTHERAPY

Doctors may also treat cancer with chemicals. This is called **chemotherapy**. About 650,000 people in the United States undergo chemotherapy each year.

There are about 100 medicines that can keep cancers from growing. There are two types of chemotherapy. One type is given as a pill or a shot. The other type is the IV line. This is a tube that puts medicine into a person's body. The tube is often placed in a vein in the arm. The IV line may also be placed in other areas of the body, such as in the chest.

The doctor makes a schedule to give chemotherapy to a cancer patient. The schedule includes times when a patient gets treatment. It also has times when the patient rests between treatments. The treatment may last days, weeks, or months.

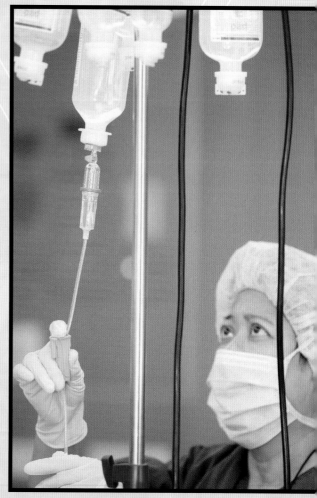

▲ A doctor adjusts IV equipment.

chemotherapy—treatment of disease, such as cancer, using chemicals

SARAH, THE SURVIVOR

Sarah found out she had cancer when she was in fourth grade. When doctors decided to treat it with chemotherapy, Sarah's mother sprang into action. She held a hair-cutting party to deal with Sarah's hair loss. This helped Sarah's friends get used to seeing her with short hair. It took some time, but Sarah's hair did fall out. Sarah got used to that.

Other things changed too, such as Sarah's taste buds. Everything began to taste like metal. She did not want to eat. She also became tired and took lots of naps. But she never gave up. After some treatment, Sarah learned that her cancer had shrunk. Finally the cancer disappeared. Sarah's taste buds returned to normal, and her hair grew back!

Side Effects of Chemotherapy

tiredness	sore mouth
hair loss	lack of appetite
nausea	

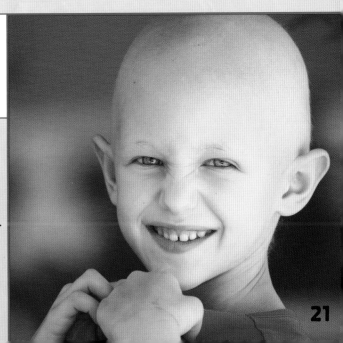

▶ Hair loss can be a side effect of cancer treatment.

RADIATION

Radiation is a third cancer treatment. It is used on about 50 percent of all cancer patients. Radiation is energy that comes from machines such as X-rays. This energy is powerful enough to slow or stop cells from growing. Radiation damages normal cells and cancer cells. Normal cells can usually repair themselves, while cancer cells cannot.

Radiation can be given in two ways. Some people receive a beam of radiation on the part of their body affected by cancer. Other people might have radioactive material placed inside their body near a cancer. The material might be solid or liquid.

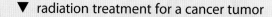
▼ radiation treatment for a cancer tumor

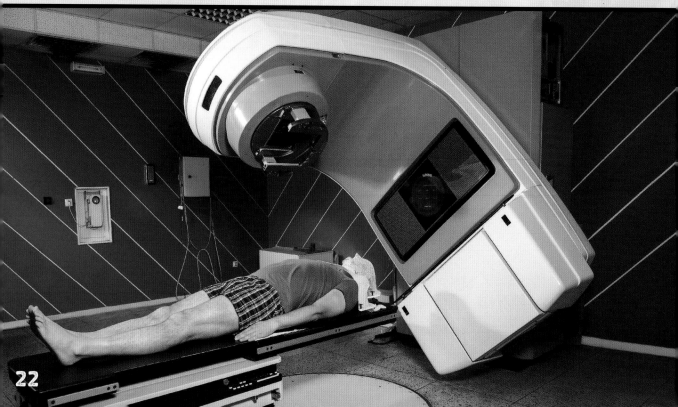

NEW FRONTIERS IN CANCER MEDICINES

Holistic medicine goes beyond just treating a person for cancer. This type of treatment focuses on the whole person—mentally, physically, and socially. It includes helping the person to eat healthier and to deal with stress. This makes the person's body, spirit, and mind feel better.

Vaccines help prevent viruses. Some are being developed today that can treat cancers people already have or help keep them from getting certain types of cancers in the future.

Someday we may be able to fight cancer with blood cell treatments. The patient's blood would be removed and treated to grow cancer-fighting cells. The treated blood would then be returned into the person's body to help fight the cancer.

▼ Some people practice yoga to deal with stress caused by cancer.

CHAPTER 4
FIGHTING CANCER

Fighting cancer is tough. Treatments require time and a lot of energy. They can also cost a lot of money.

But the things most people notice are the side effects of the treatments. Different treatments have different side effects. Some side effects can be physical, and others can be emotional.

PHYSICAL SIDE EFFECTS

When people have chemotherapy, they may experience differences in their body. Some may lose their appetite. Or they may lose their hair. Patients may also get rashes and sore throats. Some get swollen hands and feet. Some have nail and skin problems.

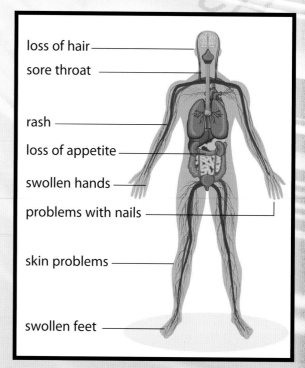

loss of hair

sore throat

rash

loss of appetite

swollen hands

problems with nails

skin problems

swollen feet

▲ physical side effects of cancer treatment

EMOTIONAL SIDE EFFECTS

Cancer patients also must deal with different emotions during treatment. They may feel tired. They may feel worried and depressed. They may feel sad or angry. They may feel nervous. It is normal to have such emotions. It is important for patients to talk about these feelings.

Emotional Side Effects of Cancer Treatment		
tiredness	depression	anger
anxiety/worry	sadness	nervousness

▼ Being sad or depressed is normal during cancer treatment.

COPING WITH CANCER

People who have cancer often need help to cope with their illness. Sometimes they may feel alone. Friends and family members may be afraid to talk to them or may avoid them altogether. But people with cancer need the support of their friends and family more than ever.

▼ Family support is important during cancer treatment.

People who have cancer should ask questions about their disease. They should also talk about their feelings. Cancer patients can join groups with other people who have been treated for cancer. These support groups allow cancer patients to meet people who have had similar experiences.

▶ Support groups help people cope with cancer.

SHANON'S STORY

In 1991 Shanon was in eighth grade when she found out she had cancer. Coping proved to be a big challenge. Shanon had many treatments and felt tired all the time. She missed many of the events she had looked forward to, such as her school play. However things changed when she went to a camp for kids with cancer. She found that spending time with kids who knew what she was going through helped her cope. It proved to be her "bright spot." In time she beat cancer. The experience led her to become a nurse.

MAKING A DIFFERENCE

Amazing things have been done to help fight cancer around the world. Part of the success is due to people who raise money for cancer research. Special walks, telethons, and other fund-raisers have raised billions of dollars for cancer research. This money goes to hospitals and research labs where cancer treatments are tested and improved.

▼ Breast cancer survivors march before the annual Koman Race for the Cure in St. Louis on June 14, 2014.

Raising money is the first step toward finding a cure for cancer. Three ways all people can help end cancer are by learning more, helping others cope, and raising awareness. In the end, everyone benefits. With each dollar raised, scientists come closer to new cures for cancer.

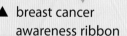

▲ breast cancer awareness ribbon

▲ Alexandra Scott

ALEX'S LEMONADE STAND

Alex's Lemonade Stand is a charity started by Alexandra Scott. She was diagnosed with cancer right before her first birthday. She received many treatments. She also vowed to raise money to help other children with cancer. When she was 4 years old, Alex started her first lemonade stand with her brother. They raised $2,000. This is one way ordinary people are making a difference in the search for a cancer cure.

Alex passed away in August 2004. She was only 8 years old. She had helped to raise more than $1 million. Her family and supporters around the world continue her legacy through Alex's Lemonade Stand Foundation.

GLOSSARY

biopsy (BYE-op-see)—taking a sample tissue to determine if it has a disease

cell (SEL)—the smallest unit of a living thing

chemotherapy (kee-moh-THER-uh-pee)—treatment of disease, such as cancer, using chemicals

CT/CAT scan (SEE-TEE/KAT SKAN)—an X-ray machine that takes pictures inside a person; CT stands for computed tomography

diagnose (dy-ig-NOHS)—to find the cause of a problem

DNA (dee-en-AY)—material in cells that gives people their individual characteristics; DNA stands for deoxyribonucleic acid

gene (JEEN)—a tiny unit of a cell that determines the characteristics that a baby gets from his or her parents

gland (GLAND)—an organ that either produces chemicals or allows substances to leave the body

lymph system (LIMF SIS-tem)—a body system that helps keep body fluids balanced and fight infections

MRI (EM-AR-EYE)—a machine that uses a magnet to help take a picture of the inside of a person; MRI stands for magnetic resonance imaging

organ (OR-guhn)—a body part that does a certain job, such as the heart or lungs

tissue (TISH-yoo)—a mass of cells that form a certain part or organ of a person, animal, or plant

tumor (TOO-mur)—an unhealthy mass of cells in the body

READ MORE

Glader, Sue. *Nowhere Hair*. Sausalito, Calif.: Thousand Words Press, 2010.

Schwartz, Heather E. *Make Good Choices: Your Guide to Making Healthy Decisions*. Healthy Me. Mankato, Minn.: Capstone Press, 2012.

Simons, Rae. *A Kid's Guide to Cancer*. Understanding Disease and Wellness. New York: Village Earth Press, 2013.

Vickers, Rebecca. *Promoting Health and Preventing Disease*. The Environment Challenge. Chicago: Raintree, 2011.

INTERNET SITES

FactHound offers a safe, fun way to find Internet sites related to this book. All of the sites on FactHound have been researched by our staff.

Here's all you do:

Visit *www.facthound.com*

Type in this code: 9781491448311

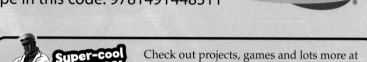

Super-cool stuff!

Check out projects, games and lots more at
www.capstonekids.com

INDEX